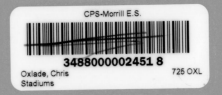

W9-BJK-199

DATE DUE

BUILDING AMAZING STRUCTURES

Stadiums

NEW EDITION

Chris Oxlade

Heinemann Library
Chicago, Illinois

Designed by Celia Floyd and Richard Parker (2nd edition)
Illustrations by Barry Atkinson
Originated by Modern Age
Printed and bound in China by WKT Company Ltd

10 09 08 07 06
10 9 8 7 6 5 4 3 2 1

Library of Congress Cataloging-in-Publication Data
Oxlade, Chris.
  Stadiums / Chris Oxlade.-- 2nd ed.
    p. cm. -- (Building amazing structures)
  Includes bibliographical references and index.
  ISBN 1-4034-7905-4 (library binding-hardcover)
  1. Stadiums--Design and construction--Juvenile literature. 2. Stadiums--History--Juvenile literature. I. Title.
II. Series.
  TH4711.O95 2006
  725'.827--dc22

                          2005024039

Acknowledgments
The publishers would like to thank the following for permission to reproduce photographs: Corbis pp. **5**, **23**, **29**; Eye Ubiquitous p. **22** (Sean Aidan); Frank Spooner p. **27**; Hutchison Library pp. **8** (Bernard Regent), **17** (Adrian Evans); J. Allan Cash Ltd pp. **14**, **20**, **21a**, **21b**, **28**; James Davis Travel Photography p. **13**; Mary Evans Picture Library p. **25**; Robert Harding p. **4**; Tony Stone pp. **6** (Jean Pragen), **11** (John Edwards), **24** (Paul Chesley); The Builder Group pp. **16**, **18**, **19**.

Cover photograph of the Allianz Arena football stadium in Munich, Germany reproduced with permission of Getty Images (Bongarts/Sandra Behene).

Every effort has been made to contact copyright holders of any material reproduced in this book. Any omissions will be rectified in subsequent printings if notice is given to the publishers.

The paper used to print this book came from sustainable resources.

The publishers and authors have done their best to ensure the accuracy and currency of all the information in this book, however, they can accept no responsibility for any loss, injury, or inconvenience sustained as a result of information or advice contained in the book.

Contents

Some words are shown in bold, **like this**. You can find out what they mean by looking in the glossary.

About Stadiums

A stadium is made up of an **arena** where events take place, and surrounding **stands** from which spectators watch the action. Most stadiums have huge roofs that cover the stands and sometimes the whole arena, too.

A stadium is a type of structure. A structure is a thing that resists a push or a pull. A stadium is a structure because it resists the weight of the people in its stands and the weight of its roof above.

Giant spaces

Stadiums are some of the biggest **public spaces** ever built. Monster stadiums built for important sporting competitions have seats for more than 100,000 people—that's one in every hundred people in a city the size of New York. They sit in **tiered** stands as high as a 30-story building.

So what types of stadiums are there? How are they built? And what materials and special machines are needed?

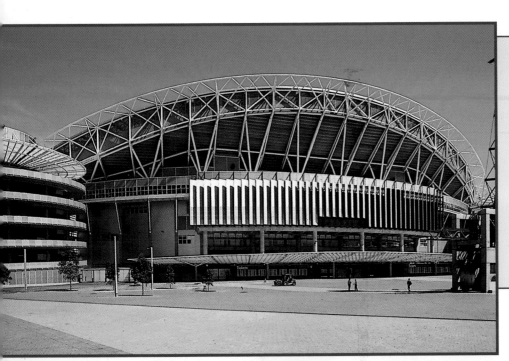

This stadium in Sydney, Australia, was built for the 2000 Olympic Games. Inside are seats for 111,000 spectators.

Why do we build stadiums?

The main reason is for sporting events. Some stadiums are built by sports teams, such as football or baseball teams, as a permanent home. Many colleges and universities also build stadiums for their teams. But most of the world's largest stadiums are built by city authorities or governments specially for a single event, such as the Olympic Games. Later, they are used for important national or international events, from sports to concerts. They must be used to pay back the hundreds of millions of dollars they cost to build.

FACTS ✣ Fixed and flexible stadiums

- The Maracana Stadium in Rio de Janeiro, Brazil has a capacity of 150,000. It would take that many people two and a half days to walk through a single door! The Circus Maximus in Ancient Rome was bigger, with a capacity for 250,000.
- The Allianz Arena in Munich, Germany can change color to suit the team that is playing in it. It was built for the soccer World Cup in 2006.
- The Beijing National Stadium for the 2008 Olympic Games in China has 80,000 permanent seats, and 20,000 temporary seats can be added when needed.

Arlington Ballpark in Texas was purpose-built as the home of the Texas Rangers baseball team.

Stadiums in the Past

More than 3,000 years ago the Ancient Greeks built the first stadiums for important events such as the ancient Olympic Games, which were always held at Olympia. Greek stadiums were longer and thinner than modern stadiums, with a simple track in the **arena** where races and combat sports such as wrestling took place. Spectators sat on embankments, which were often natural hillsides. At Olympia there was space for more than 30,000 people.

Two thousand years after it was built, you can still see the sloping seat supports in the central arena of Rome's Colosseum.

The colossal Colosseum

Roman **engineers** built stadiums known as circuses and amphitheaters. The sausage-shaped circus was for horse-racing. The extraordinary Circus Maximus in Rome was the biggest stadium ever built. It was 2,000 feet (610 meters) long, 623 feet (190 meters) wide, and could hold 250,000 spectators. It could have swallowed up four modern Olympic stadiums!

Amphitheaters had round or oval arenas with banks of seating all around. They were the venues for entertainment such as bloody gladiator fights. The greatest amphitheater was the Colosseum in Rome, completed in A.D. 82. Up to 55,000 Roman citizens sat in four **tiers** of seats, supported by rows of **columns** and arches built with brick, stone and **concrete**. The outer wall was as high as a twelve-storey building. Under the wooden arena floor was a maze of passages with an elaborate system of elevators, ramps, and trap doors to let gladiators and wild animals into the arena. Spectators were protected from the hot sun by a canvas roof called the *velarium*, supported on ropes strung above the arena.

Ancient stadium facts

The word "stadium" comes from a Greek measurement called a *stade*, which was about 623 feet (190 meters). It was the standard length of a race. A stadium was a place where people watched a stade race.

Roman engineers used pieces of volcanic rock called **pumice** in the concrete in the Colosseum. Pumice contains air bubbles, making it very light, so the weight of the structure was reduced.

Stadium Structures

All modern stadiums have a similar structure. Seats are supported by **concrete** slabs, which are supported by a strong **steel** or concrete frame. The frame rests on **foundations** under the ground. The frame also supports the floors inside the stadium.

Finding a firm base

Deep underground there is always hard, solid rock, which is called **bedrock**. Sometimes the bedrock reaches right to the surface, but normally it is covered with layers of softer rocks, such as clay, and a layer of very soft topsoil.

If the bedrock is near the surface, the soft soil is removed and concrete foundations for the frame are built on top of the rock. If the bedrock is deeper down, steel or concrete **columns** called **piles** reach down through the softer layers to the bedrock beneath. The columns of the frame rest on top of the piles.

Sometimes the bedrock is too deep for piles to reach. In this case the frame rests on a large **reinforced concrete** slab foundation which spreads its weight into the ground.

Cantilevered upper tiers of seating, free of supporting columns, give spectators a clear view of the arena.

Members of the frame

The frame is made up of **members**. **Horizontal** members called **beams** support seating and floors. **Vertical** members called columns support the beams and the roof. The seating slabs and floors are made of reinforced concrete and supported at their edges by the beams of the frame. The external walls, made from **cladding** materials, hang on the outside of the frame.

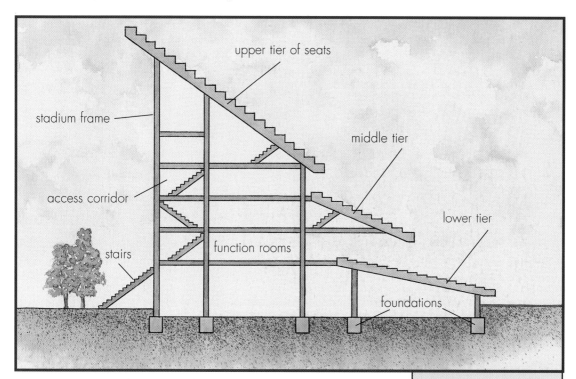

upper tier of seats

middle tier

stadium frame

lower tier

access corridor

stairs

function rooms

foundations

TRY THIS

Supporting a cantilevered stand
Hold one end of a pen firmly in a clenched fist. While holding the pen in a horizontal position, press down on the other end of the pen. The press represents the weight of the people in their seats and your fist represents the frame in the stand. Can you feel how the support (your fist) needs to push down in one place and push up in another to stop the cantilever (pen) from falling?

This is a cross-section of a stadium stand. The tiers are angled so that spectators can see the near side of the arena.

Stadium Roofs

Stadiums have some of the biggest roofs ever built. Some roofs protect just the spectators from the sun and rain. Others stretch right across the **arena**, creating an indoor stadium. A few stadiums have roofs with sliding sections which can be closed in bad weather. Stadium roofs are always supported from behind or above to avoid having columns that would block spectators' views.

The Toronto Sky Dome in Canada has an enormous sliding roof. Here it is in the opened position.

Cantilevers and cables

In a **cantilever** roof, **beams** attached to the back edge of the stand stretch out over the seating. They support thin sheets of roofing material, such as **steel**. **Cable-stay** roofs are supported from above by steel cables or bars attached to tall masts.

Steel roof beams are normally in the form of structures called **trusses**. Trusses are also used to make roof structures stiff so that they do not flap about in strong winds.

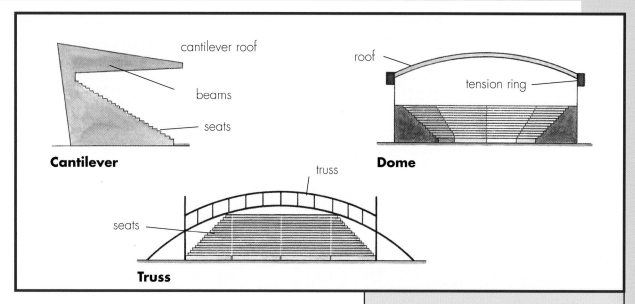

Completely over the top

The most spectacular stadium roofs are those of giant indoor stadiums, which span more than 650 feet (200 meters) without any support. There are only a few of these in the world. Some roofs are huge domes.The weight of the roof goes around the dome shape to its rim. The weight tries to push the rim outwards, so the rim needs to be supported. One way is to use a steel structure a called a **tension** ring, which is like a band that stretches right around the stadium, keeping the rim fromspreading outwards.

The roof of the Pontiac Silverdome in Michigan has no supports at all! It is kept up by air. The roof is made of thin plastic, kept in place by wires stretched across the stadium. Huge fans keep the **air pressure** inside the stadium slightly higher than outside, which lifts the roof.

TRY THIS
Shapes for strength
If you hold a flat piece of paper horizontally by one edge, the other edge flops down. But hold the edge in a valley-shaped curve, and the flimsy paper becomes a structure. Amazing! This channel shape is used for some stadium roofs.

Stadium Materials

Many different construction materials are used in stadiums, including metals, bricks and stone, glass, and plastics. But the main materials in stadium structures are **concrete** and **steel**, which are used to build **foundations**, frames and roofs.

Steel frames and trusses

Steel is an **alloy** made mostly of iron. Steel is used to make cables, the **members** of steel frames, and roof **trusses**. It is extremely strong. For example, a steel cable as thick as your finger could lift a 30-ton truck without snapping.

Mixing concrete

Concrete is made by mixing **cement**, water and aggregate, which consists of sand and gravel or stone chips. When the ingredients are first put together, the concrete is runny. The cement reacts with the water and they harden into a solid which holds the aggregate together.

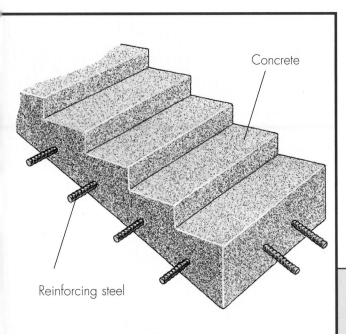

Concrete

Reinforcing steel

If you try to stretch concrete, it cracks quite easily. So the concrete used to make a part of a stadium that will be stretched needs to be strengthened. Steel bars are added to the concrete and this new material is called **reinforced concrete**.

This is a simplified diagram of a section of reinforced concrete used for seating.

Light but strong

The covering materials for stadium roofs must be waterproof and strong, but also lightweight because they have to be held up by the roof structure. Apart from metal sheets, roof builders use plastics and special fabrics containing glass fibres for strength. Sometimes these are transparent to allow natural light into the stadium.

The extraordinary roofs of the Olympic Park and athletics stadium in Munich, Germany are made of plastic supported by cables and wires.

TRY THIS

Cracker beams

You can make a reinforced **beam** from a cracker (the concrete) and paper (the steel)! Use the longest, thinnest, flattest cracker you can find. Cut a piece of paper the same shape as the cracker and glue it underneath the cracker. Lay the cracker like a bridge between two books and press in the middle until it breaks. Compare its strength to a cracker on its own, without the paper.

13

Designing a Stadium

Before construction of a stadium starts, an organization asks a company of **architects** to design the stadium for them. It tells the architects how many spectators the stadium needs to hold, what mixture of events will take place, and whether it wants a complete or sliding roof.

Architects often present their ideas the form of a model. This model shows the plans for the new Yankee Stadium in New York.

Working out loads

An architect starts by drawing some rough sketches of his or her ideas for the shape and style of the new stadium. After the ideas are presented to the client, the design becomes more detailed. Next, a **structural engineer** designs the structure. The stadium structure needs to support the weight of the people in the **stands**—called the live **loads** – and the weight of the parts of the stadium itself – called the dead loads.

Safety and comfort

Stadium designers must also design doorways, corridors, elavators, and steps. These will allow spectators to reach their seats quickly and safely before an event and to leave again afterwards. Big stadiums can hold more people than live in a small city, and they need facilities such as snack bars and cafés. A 75,000-seat stadium needs 800 toilets! So like any other building, a stadium needs **services**, such as water, electricity, gas, and communications (for example, telephone lines).

All the details of a stadium are stored on computer, which can show what the stadium will look like from any angle.

A large team of designers and **engineers** is needed to do all of the design work. Once the design is complete, drawings and plans are prepared for the people who will build the stadium.

Facilities for the disabled

Modern stadiums must have facilities for people with disabilities. These include ramps and lifts for wheelchairs, signs that can be read by touch, special toilets, and devices called hearing loops that allow blind people to listen to in-stadium commentaries.

Starting a Stadium

Building a stadium takes several years and involves hundreds of people. One **engineering** company—the main contractor—organizes the whole project and may do some of the work. The specialist jobs, such as installing floodlights, are done by smaller companies called sub-contractors.

Laying foundations

The first stage in laying the **foundations** is to remove any soft topsoil from the site. This is done by excavating machines and dump trucks that carry the soil away. If a slab foundation is being used, reinforcing **steel** is put in place and **concrete** is poured round it until the concrete reaches the correct depth. Steel is left sticking out of the concrete for the frame to be attached to.

The frame must be constructed next, because it supports all the other parts of the stadium. The very bottom sections of the frame are connected to the foundations.

Here you can see the concrete frame of a new **stand** under construction. In the foreground are roof supports.

Pieces of a jigsaw

The **members** of a steel frame are made up of flat pieces of steel **welded** together and cut to the correct length. They are prefabricated in a factory and delivered to the site. There they are put together like a giant jigsaw puzzle, with high-strength nuts and bolts or by welding.

Massive moulds

Concrete frames are normally built *in situ* (on site) by pouring concrete into wooden or metal molds called **formwork**. Bars of steel reinforcement are put inside the formwork and the concrete is poured around them. Bars are left poking out of the **beams** and **columns** for the next sections to be attached to.

This picture was taken during the building of the Olympic Stadium in Barcelona, Spain. On the right you can see the arm of a concrete pump.

Mechanical helpers

All the materials for a frame, such as steel beams and columns, and concrete for the floors, have to be lifted to where they are needed. Tall construction cranes do most of the lifting. Fresh, runny concrete is lifted by cranes in huge containers, or pumped up in pipes.

Floors, Roofs, and Services

As the frame of the stadium takes shape, work starts on the **concrete** floors, staircases and seating slabs.

Pouring floors and seats

Internal floors and seating slabs are made from **reinforced concrete**. They carry the weight of the spectators to the frame. Floors are made by laying special steel plates side by side, with their ends connected to the beams, to make a steel deck. Then concrete is poured on to the deck. Seating slabs are made by placing **pre-cast** reinforced concrete beams next to each other, or by pouring concrete into **formwork** molds. Reinforcing steel is placed in the mold before the concrete is poured around it.

Cladding is attached to the outside of the frame to make the walls. It might be brickwork, huge panes of glass, or thin sheets of metal.

In this frame of a roof under construction, the red pieces are temporary supports.

Adding the roof

When the structure of the stands is complete, the roof can be added. Temporary supports may be needed to hold up the parts until the roof structure can support itself. Roof panels are added when the roof framework is complete.

Installing services

Dozens of sub-contractors move into the empty stadium to start installing water pipes, electricity cables, toilets, catering equipment, and so on.

Hard-wearing plastic seats are bolted to the completed reinforced concrete slabs.

FACTS ✤ Shopping list for the Millennium Stadium, Wales, UK (1999)
- 1,350 **piles**
- 40,000 tons of concrete—that would take you about 30 years to mix by hand!
- 4,000 tons of reinforcing steel bars
- 12,000 tons of steel for the frame and roof
- 29,000 square yards (24,000 square meters) of cladding—enough to cover the pitch in the arena five times.

Stadiums in Use

Dozens of people are needed to maintain the stadium and to make it run smoothly, from groundspeople who take care of the **arena**, to electricians who service the floodlights. Stadiums are not used every day. In fact, some are used only a few days every month. So stadiums are either very full or nearly empty!

Coping with crowds

When an event takes place, hundreds of staff are needed – ushers to control crowds, caterers to make food, and cleaners to tidy up afterwards. The spectators all need to get into their seats quickly and safely. People enter the stadium through gates called turnstiles, where the stadium authorities check tickets and count how many people have entered the stadium. After the event, the rush is even greater because everybody leaves at once, so large exit doors are opened.

Tens of thousands of spectators arrive at the stadium in the few hours before an event starts.

All change in the stadium

A few indoor stadiums have been specially designed to hold different events. In these amazing stadiums, the lower **tiers** of seats are movable so that the size of the **arena** can be changed and different numbers of people seated. For example, on one day a stadium can hold a baseball game on a full-sized field, and a few days later a pop concert on a stage, with the seating moved back.

Here is Toronto's Sky Dome with the arena arranged for football ...

… and re-arranged, with temporary stands, for a tennis tournament.

In an emergency

Stadiums have emergency medical rooms staffed by people qualified in first aid, where minor injuries can be treated. For big events there may be an ambulance standing by, too. With so many people crowded into a stadium, fire is the worst hazard, although modern stadiums are very well fireproofed. If fire does break out, public address announcements are made, and ushers and clear signs direct people to the exits. If the electricity fails, it could make it difficult for people to leave the stadium, so generators spring into action to provide emergency lighting.

21

Making Space Indoors

Stadiums are not the only structures that create huge spaces where people can gather for events. Other buildings with huge indoor spaces include exhibition halls, factories and places of worship, such as cathedrals. As with stadiums, the roofs of these buildings are designed with as few supports inside the buildings as possible. Buildings with roofs more than about 33 yards (30 meters) wide without a support are called long-span buildings.

Radical roofs

Small roofs are supported by roof **trusses** stretching from wall to wall. Trusses support thin metal or plastic sheets. The weight from the roof is transferred to the ends of the trusses and down **columns** to the **foundations**. Longer roof spans are made possible by supporting the roof trusses by using cables connected to towers. These roofs are called **cable-stay** roofs.

London's Millenium Dome is not a true dome. It has a cable-stay roof supported by a ring of gigantic towers.

Some huge roofs are made with thin slabs of **reinforced concrete**. The strength of **concrete** roofs comes from their special curved shapes. Concrete roofs can be incredibly thin. For example, the top of a concrete dome 109 yards (100 meters) across can be just 0.8 inch (2 centimeters) thick.

Other roofs are supported by wires strung from one side of a building to the other, like the cables of a suspension bridge. One type of cable roof is shaped like a bicycle wheel on its side. Madison Square Garden arena in New York has this sort of roof.

The fabric of the Minneapolis Metrodome is supported by air pressure inside the building. Steel wires keep the fabric in place.

Roofs over towns

Some **architects** have suggested that modern materials and building methods could be used to create roofs far larger than any stadium roof—big enough to cover a small town. Under the roof, people could live in a perfect climate, protected from bad weather.

Vaults and Domes

The builders of ancient structures did not have super-strong materials such as **steel**, so they could not make huge roof structures like those we have today. Gradually, though, they developed ways of making roofs to cover big spaces.

Vaults and domes

The first permanent roof structure was called a barrel **vault**, which is like half a cylinder on its side. The Ancient Egyptians knew how to build barrel vaults, and the Ancient Romans used them for many public buildings. But a barrel vault is like a tunnel—it is gloomy because light can only get in at the two ends! The Romans also invented a new type of vault called a groin vault, made of two barrel vaults at right angles to each other. This was supported at four corners, so light could get into the building between the supports at the corners.

The dome of the Pantheon was completed in A.D. 128. It is 141 feet (43 meters) wide. Roman **engineers** made it entirely of **concrete**, with no reinforcement.

Vaults and domes were used in many religious buildings in the **Middle Ages**, such as the huge Gothic cathedrals of Europe. In these cathedrals, the outer walls are enormously high—up to ten stories. The outwards push from the vaults would topple walls this high over, so the walls themselves are supported by more walls called buttresses and flying buttresses. This allowed huge stained-glass windows to go into the walls, too. These amazing roofs were built completely by hand.

TRY THIS

Egg-streme strength

Next time you have an egg, keep the shell as whole as you can. Carefully break away one end of the shell to leave a dome shape. Stand the dome on a flat surface and press on the top. You might be surprised at how hard you have to press to break the shell. It's because the shell is a dome, which gets its strength from its shape, even though the shell is thin and brittle.

The Crystal Palace, London, built in 1851, had an iron supporting frame and enough glass to cover 15 football fields.

Stadium Disasters

Modern stadiums safely support the **stands** where the spectators sit, and the roofs that protect them from the weather. Stadiums are designed to withstand strong winds, heavy snow and earthquakes. But there have been some terrible accidents caused by poor design and crowd control.

Crowd disasters

HILLSBOROUGH In 1989, hundreds of soccer fans rushed into a stand at the Hillsborough stadium in Sheffield, England, to catch the start of a big game. Fans at the front of the terraced stand, which had no seats, were crushed against a security fence. Over 200 people were injured and 96 were killed. This disaster led to new rules for large British stadiums. Standing areas and security fences were banned.

IBROX Near the end of a soccer match in 1971 at Ibrox Park, Glasgow, Scotland, fans leaving the ground early tried to turn back because of a last-minute goal. People fell down a wide, steep stairway, crushing those below. Over 150 fans were injured, and 66 died. In 1982, more than three hundred fans died in a similar accident at the Lenin Stadium in Moscow. Other crush disasters have been caused by fans trying to escape from riots.

Fires

BRADFORD In 1985, a fire at the grounds of Bradford City Football Club in England killed 56 people. The stadium's wooden stand was 77 years old and had piles of trash under it. Fire swept through it in five minutes, trapping the victims. As a result fire regulations were improved at other grounds.

Service and structure collapses

NEW ORLEANS In 2005, more than 20,000 people sheltered from Hurricane Katrina in the Louisiana Superdome. Parts of the roof blew off and the electricity and other **services** failed, causing massive problems of safety, security, and comfort.

BASTIA In 1992, 15 spectators died and over 2,000 were injured in the French town of Bastia when a temporary stand collapsed as spectators filled it before a soccer match.

Here you can see the remains of the temporary stand at Bastia, in France.

Stadium Facts

FACTS ✦ Modern stadiums with largest capacities*

STADIUM	CAPACITY	DATE
• Maracana, Rio de Janeiro, Brazil	150,000	1950
• Mineirao, Belo Horizonte, Brazil	130,000	1970
• Salt Lake Stadium, Calcutta, India	120,000	1984
• Azteca Stadium, Mexico City, Mexico	114,000	1966
• Sydney Olympic Stadium, Australia	110,000	1999

* Stadium capacities rise and fall constantly as new stands are added or standing areas are converted to seating.

This is the enormous bowl of the Maracana Stadium, Rio de Janeiro, Brazil.

FACTS ✦ Massive indoor stadiums

STADIUM	CAPACITY	DATE
• Silverdome, Pontiac, Michigan	80,400	1980
• Astrodome, Houston, Texas	74,000	1965
• Millennium Stadium, Cardiff, Wales, UK	72,500	1999

FACTS ❖ History's important stadiums
- 4th century BC Circus Maximus, Rome. Biggest stadium ever (250,000).
- A.D. 82 The Colosseum, Rome. First true stadium with seating in **tiers**.
- 1896 Olympic stadium, Athens. First stadium for modern Olympics.
- 1908 Shepherd's Bush stadium, London. First modern purpose-built stadium.
- 1959 Dodger Stadium, Los Angeles, USA. First tiered stadium with no supporting **columns**.
- 1964 Shea Stadium, New York. First multi-use stadium.
- 1965 Astrodome, Houston, Texas. First large indoor stadium.
- 1989 Toronto Sky Dome, Canada. First stadium with **retractable dome**.

FACTS ❖ More stadium facts
- Tallest floodlight towers: Melbourne Cricket Ground, Australia. Height: 246 feet (75 meters).
- Largest roof by area: Munich Olympic Stadium, Germany. Area:102,000 square yards (85,000 square meters)—equal to 19 football fields.
- Largest **concrete** dome: King Dome, Seattle, Washington. Diameter: 660 feet (201 meters).

The Astrodome in Houston, Texas has seats for 66,000 spectators under its plastic roof, which is supported by a **lattice** of steel.

Glossary

Stadia or stadiums?
Either word, *stadia* or *stadiums*, can be used to mean "more than one stadium". In this book we use *stadiums*.

air pressure   pressure created by air. Air pressure keeps balloons and tires inflated.

alloy   material made of a metal combined with another metal or other substance

architect   person who designs the shape, appearance, and internal layout of a building

arena   central area of a stadium, where events take place

beam   length of steel or concrete supported at both ends

bedrock   layers of hard, solid rock that are found in the Earth's surface and continue deep into the Earth's crust

cable-stay   structure supported from above by cables

cantilever   beam supported at just one of its ends

capacity   number of spectators that can fit into a stadium

cement   mixture of chemicals that hardens into a rock-like substance after it is mixed with water

cladding   material used to make the external wall of a stadium or other modern building

column   vertical member of a frame, which carries load downwards

concrete   very hard material made up of cement, water, and aggregate

engineer   person who designs or builds structures

formwork   metal or wooden mold that concrete is poured into

foundation   structure that spreads the weight of a stadium and the people in it into the ground

gladiator   person who fought to the death for public entertainment in Ancient Rome

horizontal   flat, or from side to side, not up and down

lattice   pattern made by crossed bars or strips laid diagonally, with spaces between

load   any force that acts on a structure, such as the weight of the people in its stands or the weight of the water on its roof

member   piece of a frame, such as a beam or a column

Middle Ages   time in European history between A.D. 500 and 1500

30

pile long steel or concrete pole driven deep into the ground

pre-cast set into a shape before being put in place on the structure

public space building or area where people gather for events, such as stadiums and exhibition halls

pumice rock formed from lava that comes out of a volcano and then cools and sets

reinforced concrete concrete that has steel reinforcing (strengthening) bars embedded in it

retractable dome roof that can move so that the stadium is either covered or uncovered

services electricity, water, elevators, communications, and other such items that are needed by the spectators and all the people working in a stadium

stand area of raised seating from which spectators watch the action in the arena

steel type of very strong metal made mostly of iron

structural engineer engineer who designs the structure of a building

tension force that pulls on opposite sides of an object, trying to stretch it

tier single level of seating in a stand. Some stands have three or even four tiers, one above the other.

truss beam made up of a framework of steel members bolted or welded together

vault arched or domed roof or ceiling

venue location where an event takes place

vertical upright, straight up and down

welded attach two pieces of metal to each other by heating them until they melt, then joining them together

More Books to Read

Good, Keith. *Build it!: Super Structures*. Minneapolis, Minn.: Lerner Publishing Group, 1999.

Owens, Thomas. *Sports Palaces: Football Stadiums*. New York: Millbrook Press, 2001.

Wilkinson, Philip. *Amazing Buildings*. New York: Dorling Kindersley Publishing, 1992.

Index